Spit Out the Myth

Danaé Wellington
Silé Sibanda
Warda Yassin

the poetry business

Published 2023 by
The Poetry Business
Campo House,
54 Campo Lane,
Sheffield S1 2EG

ISBN 978-1-914914-61-4
eBook ISBN 978-1-914914-62-1

Designed and typeset by Utter
Printed by Biddles Books

'A Sonnet for Sheffield' by Warda Yassin commissioned
by Orchard Square

Smith|Doorstop Books are a member of Inpress:
www.inpressbooks.co.uk

Distributed by BookSource, 50 Cambuslang Road,
Cambuslang Investment Park, Glasgow G32 8NB.

The Poetry Business gratefully acknowledges
the support of Arts Council England.

Supported by
**ARTS COUNCIL
ENGLAND**

Contents

5   Introduction

Poems by Danaé Wellington

8   The Last Day with Maria

10   Poco Woman

12   Wednesday Night

14   Heritage

16   The Mothers: Retirement, St. Elizabeth, 1792

17   Dis Poem

19   An Ode To Blackbirds That Keep On Dreaming

20   The Spirits Talk

Poems By Silé Sibanda

22   Simple things of Life

23   Zimbabwe

24   Loving from a distance

25   Torn

26   When God Judges me

27   You Faded

Poems by Warda Yassin

30   Cavendish Court

32   A Sonnet for Sheffield

33   Somaliland

34   Summer of Year 9

35   What Ahmed told me in GCSE English

36   The Glow Up

37   When Andrea comes to paint me

INTRODUCTION

Writing a forward for any book is a great responsibility, it sets the tone for what you're about to read, it delivers a frame that you can rest in, it opens the door so you can peek through and know what to expect.

This collection will not deliver what you expect but exactly what you need.

Three amazing poets, who have been in each other's company through lifetimes (this is not the first time their work appears together. Mentored by poet Vicky Morris at Hive, which has supported so many young poets in the city and given them a place to be). There is an experience together here. They speak of the lands they came from and the lands they live in now. They speak to liberation movements and what could be.

I was guest curating for Off The Shelf the year Jean Binta Breeze died. And it struck me how much we were losing and what it means to live in that loss when it's too late to do or say or hear them. It feels as though silencing follows Black Women, ready, when they were once loud and then so quickly not there. I searched to see what books were available of Jean's and it saddened me that so many are out of print. It was the same when I sought out Grace Nicholls for the same event. Let's not wait til they can't hear us in the same way we hear them. I asked these three poets, Danaé Wellington, Warda Yassin and Silé Sibanda to craft a response, if they wouldn't mind honouring her words and life as a poet that spoke to a particular time, a very specific moment in the evolution of Blackness and Britishness and words. Some had met and already shared a stage with Jean. Three very different starting points on that journey, she meant different things to each of them. They are like backing singers who are family. They share a similar tone but do different things. Jamaica speaks to Zimbabwe speaks to Somalia, chorus in Sheffield. It is not the first time they've shared a page. Plates shared with cousins but "no guarantee of meat".

'What Ahmed told me in GCSE English' is a hammer, a beautiful reminder of what going to school can mean for some. "Check the football in the rubble."

"Beat my name into the skin of your drum ... Poco woman, sing."

Which is just what Jean Binta Breeze demanded, that we sing ourselves whole and here. And that is what these three poets have done, are doing and will continue to do. Sheffield is a writers space, a poets corner and we that live here are spoilt for choice. This collection is landscape heavy and the landscapes they describe move from there to here. Exactly one of the themes for Jean, there to here, here to there and what is lost or found along the way.

Pack your bag, put in it a compass, some cardamom tea and good cake and walk with them through that landscape. You may not miss home.

Désirée Reynolds

POEMS BY DANAÉ WELLINGTON

OFF THE SHELF FESTIVAL OF WORDS

DANAÉ WELLINGTON is a Jamaican-British poet, writer, performance artist, cultural producer and vocalist based in Sheffield. She is the founder of Odd Child Productions, a Black and neurodiverse-led events and production company. Danaé is the current Sheffield Poet Laureate (2022-2024) and has been published in several anthologies including *Halfway Smile and Surfing the Twilight* (Hive 2018/2019) and has written for Black Ballad UK. She is an alumnus of the Hive South Yorkshire network and Obsidian Foundation (2023) and has performed at a number of festivals including Ted Hughes Poetry Festival, Tramlines, Sheaf Poetry Festival, and Off the Shelf.

The Last Day with Maria

You danced in the kitchen of that
sky-blue cement house. Hips swaying to *Dos Gardenias*
for the third time –
your two-step peppering the air like a rumba.

The soursop tree stretched to catch a peek
of your mischief, as you pour pitch-black
Café Bustelo into your porcelain pot.
Your veined hands stirring love
into my sweet, condensed milk tea.

I watch you as I sip from my favourite whitecup,
ushering the warmth of you into my chest. Your olive skin a sun trap.
Moss eyes green as a bayou marshland.

You sit me down by the piano to tell me stories
of another life. Of days long gone.
Your Havana fingers lilt with an ebb and flow,
every story accompanied by forlorn. Each tale swelling with an ache
for the son you had to leave behind.
He was the sound that lived in the Putumayo records
you only played when the urge to mother swallowed you whole.

That evening,
we were on bended knees at the bedside.
The Lord's prayer perched on the edge of your lips,
a hymn that grew wings and flew.
You recited Psalms that lived beneath your tongue:

Search me, God and know my heart; test me
and know my anxious thoughts.

There was a storm brewing and you heard it coming.

When Nurse Sylvia's voice broke through,
I could hear the lump ballooning in her throat.
Her mouth only gave way for two words:
she gaan.

I pushed my way pass the humbug of grown-ups to get to your bedside.
maybe this was a game,
maybe I was your hero.
maybe it was my turn to wake you with a praise song
or a two-step riddim.
I tried to shake you back to life. But you
wouldn't budge.

You were always the bull-headed woman.

Poco Woman

Beat my name into the skin of your drum,
call me into earth.
Poco woman, sing.

Sweat line the crevices of your olive breasts,
my body bound to the blue-black sky.
Poco woman, sing.

Pull me from the moonlit belly of a river Mumma,
this child balmed in prophecy and prayer.
Feed me your milk with no shame for age,
a ritual only magic women can perform.

Let the spell move from under your finger,
chant a story of freedom come.
Poco woman, sing.

Open the doorway of your mouth, and
spit out the myth in the back of your throat.
Poco woman, sing.

You are a griot, a spiralling tunnel
teaching the sleeping children about mysteries
of love and time.
There is no distance that can separate
the heart from its home.

Tear open the veil between two worlds,
stand with parting feet and push.
Poco woman, sing.

Sing for the night women.
Sing with your centenarian body.
Sing and call down the revelations.
Sing for the shy schoolgirls and dried belly women.

Sing, Poco woman, sing.

Wednesday Night

On the red polished veranda, you'd sit
with your hands as a podium to set your bible.
Its pages dog eared, and seasoned with years of:

Hallelujah!
Amen!
Praise di Lord!

It was a tender heirloom. A buoy for daughters
threatened with drowning, and for their children,
and children's children.

You found your smile when Jerry Springer
was on daytime television. A saintly woman,
who loved a little gossip and trouble every now and again.
It tempered the years of righteousness in your step.

In that bible, browned and shapeshifting,
the scriptures knew you better than your husband.
The only affair that would warrant you a bly,
and escape the mouths of clucking church women.

On Wednesday nights,
you and the church mothers would congregate
for prayer meeting. You gathered for the Lord and went to war.
After anointing yourselves with olive oil,
you would swap secrets like:

the good starch for the khaki shirt,
the recipe for blue draws, and
Sisters Lynne's big mouth husband's carrying on.

You cackled with these women in a cacophony,
with a mouth full of bammy, coco-tea
and *hear-seh*.
To your children, you courted faith more than
any man you ever loved. A quiet, reserved house woman.

But to the Wednesday night sistrin,
you were *Sister Lurline wid di rambunctious laugh,*
a woman that love coco-tea and a little trouble
every now and again.

bly: To grant mercy or giving someone a chance without judgement or penalty in situations of
wrongdoing; turning a blind eye.

Heritage

The veiny palm of a banana leaf
carries mi in its clutch like a wanderlust guided by the wind,
it holds my body as an oracle would a prophecy.

Call dung sun,
Kromanti woman
Call dung rain,
Kromanti man

The conjuring of reckless teenagers,
a guiness and a spliff and all the weight of their dreams
in love – I watch them as they fashion mi.

Together,
dancing with ink on the bottom of their feet,
they write mi like a story onto an ivory page,
in riddim at the hips until I am a seed,
buried in the soil of my mothers womb.

Call dung fire,
Asante woman
Call dung spirit
Asante man

Unfurling against time,
I am waiting to bloom into the offspring of a nation:

Beat your drum river woman
Beat your drum river man
Ululate at the crack of dawn
Yoruba woman, clear di passage for your daughter.

Watch those river eyes shine,
see that blue mountain mouth form,
in that chest is a dying sound.
Silver back child you are the burning spear,
rebel child, you are history and heritage.

The Mothers: Retirement, St. Elizabeth, 1792

They stand in formation staunch and ready, *Amina, Nana, Odeh, Okoumfoh*,
four sisters of tyranny looking out across the sugar-cane field. An earthquake,
shaking the ground of Massa John's compound, women of cutlass and folktales.
Their girlish daughters, *Majorie, Blossom and Akin* are gathering baskets
                              full of hope,
picking swallowed dreams from the red sun-baked dirt, giggling
                              amongst themselves
in the suffocating heat.

Beads of sweat gather on the brow of the mothers. They straighten their
bending backs, iron the kinks at the end of their spine and stretch
                              towards the sky.
In ritual, they oil each other's scalp with guerilla warfare and canerow
                              toughness into
jet-black coiling hair. These women belong to themselves. They ripped
                              open their
mouths that were snapped shut and took two fingers to pluck out the
                              silence balled up
in the back of their neck. They wrap their bodies in indigo stained
                              kaliko cloth – a luxury
claimed for themselves – and ketch a myal when drummer man start
                              with a beat.

Before the night was over, the mothers would bury a box of chicken
                              feathers, rusty nails,
a yarn of cotton and baby teeth. A time-travelling vessel put to sleep deep
                              beneath the mud.
It was buried by an almond tree, an heirloom that would only emerge
                              for the daughters
delicate enough to hear their spirit cries.

Dis Poem

is for all the men that I know.
Tender brown skin swaddling survival   like boys in desperate need of love,
of hands that move shade from the darker sides of them.
Black boy
gathers his tears and cups his eyes
catching salt water to stop him from drowning
his father taught him that flowers are only a gift for goodbyes
never a welcome home.

Dis poem is for him with
softened fists
chanting Binghi man salutations
wa gwaan
yes Iya
trod good
blessed love
greetings in the name of Jah Rastafari-I
convincing himself
mi good
mi good
mi good.
He pours libations for his beloveds
devoured by time the hungry vulture.

Dis poem is for him, for them
a sea of obsidian skin
With perching feet that greet the edge of a precipice
a multitude of spirits growing restless like duppy inna dead yard.
The white man's rule of thumb
cuts them down
like a tree torn from its roots

men without a home
Black skin with no sun
an ocean song
who harbours love
and sails ships in search of freedom
beyond this first world graveyard, Babylon.

An Ode To Blackbirds That Keep On Dreaming

In this house, we frolic in an empty garden.
The only time we look over our shoulders
is to check if the sun has kept its smile for us.

Our feet would greet water, paddle it back and forth
calling it to greet us back. It would tell us
stories of the Igbo and Ashanti. Show us

Nzinga and Akua, Kofi and Quashie.
They would tell us of their children Nana and Amina,
and weave our myths in a garland of Hibiscus flowers.

There would be no-one to smite us and damn us to hell,
and our names would not be forgotten or left to rot in
the carcass of colonial history.

They would live on the island of our bodies
and summon the native tongue
from its hiding place.

In this house,
our people would be angels, black birds in flight,
our sing-song voice a hymn for the living
and our stories a praise song for the departed.

The Spirits Talk

Girl child, we hear your tears running like
a river in the night,
a commotion stirring inside your room
when we press our ear to the wall.
A louding song, a Mamiwata cry.

You thought it was us who tied him to you,
our conjuring of an agitated lover,
your accusing finger pointed to everyone
but the devil in him.

Back then, you were the contortionist
bent yourself into the home you wished he would live in,
but he was only there to pillage, ransack,
enter then leave.
You became the boarding house haunted
by stale kisses, bones covered in white sheets,
phone ringing out like an unanswered heartbeat.

Girl child, are you really full?
Gulping all those spoonfuls of shame? Sugared with years
of lusting. The one time you closed your door
he disappeared – became the ghost you only see
when you pray to forget him.

Boys like this
are bad juju. And like ghosts –
they come and they go.

POEMS BY SILÉ SIBANDA

OFF THE SHELF
FESTIVAL
OF WORDS

SILÉ SIBANDA is a spoken word performer, workshop facilitator, award-winning BBC radio presenter and events host. She has been involved in creative and community projects for over 12 years, starting with a glee club at the age of 12. Recently she has been facilitating creative writing workshops for various organisations including Grimm and Co, Artful and Creative Lives. She is an active part of the Hive Writing Collective. In 2022, Silé became a producer for the UK's largest immersive storytelling experience StoryTrails, telling untold stories of people living in Sheffield.

Simple things of Life

She sits in her brown cushioned chair
Calm
At home
Held by the land she calls her own
Drinking red bush milky tea with 3 sugars
Enjoying the simple things of life

We are playing amatope
In a ground-drawn kitchen
sand grain rice, mud leaf stew and rock meat
are perfect substitutes
for practising for our turn
when we have a place to call our own
just like gogo.

Farming in the morning
letting the cows roam free
in search of food on Zimbabwe's fertile soil.
Taking goats for a drink,
in the local water well.
Taking turns pumping out water
quenching our thirst at the same time

Laying under an acacia tree
in a dry riverbed under the mid-day sun,
in mother nature's company.
Sharing stories whilst cooking dinner
in an open fire at night
Star gazing, giving them names, a purpose.

Zimbabwe

Zimbabwe like my ex-boyfriend
was mesmerizing at the beginning
destructive at the end.

From the food to the bedroom
I was sharing with other people,
Two plates divided amongst four cousins
with no guarantee of any meat.
Trust me,
I became a savage.

With only one tv channel
one state of mind divided amongst two
turned predictable.

Playing umamchanyana
"Dodgeball" become the prime sport
I was dodging hunger
Oblivious to poverty
Preserving my youth.

Loving from a distance

His hair, a flourishing black rainforest
untamed, liana vines
spiralling out of control.
The paradise of our dreams

Building shelter there exposes you
to landmines activated by Stella,
sensitive to laughter.

Once triggered, his hands
are a truck with its brakes cut
travelling 90 miles an hour
on a residential road with houses made by us.
His mouth a shotgun,
words propelling pallets that spread out
when penetrating our hearts.
Their intention maximum damage.

Realising the destruction,
his cries are artificial crops
manufactured to increase dis-ease.
His empathy resigned,
it left a letter stating a bowl with holes
shall take its place instead.

Our only regret,
Not Loving from a distance

Torn

Torn away from home,
leaving concrete memories for unfamiliar land.
Cries replacing prayer whispered during sleep, the only place peace
                    comes for a visit.
At dawn, evicted by bullets for our interpretation of God.
Beaten for the pigment on your skin, or being born woman,
yearning to rewind time to beg for a different shade or gender.
You will pay extra for it.

When God Judges me

She is loyalty,
playing for Premier League team Family United,
defending champions of minding their own business.
Navigating the map of sisterhood,
cashing in blackmail coins for loafs of favours
sharing maximum hold hair gel and wide-leg jeans.

Defrosting insecurities with camomile tea
He walks in heart first,
wearing cloak of ancestral heritage on his tongue.
Has friendships with no strings attached
except cultivating million-door mindsets
on university soil.

Their mantra "There's no such thing as lack of abundance"
just pay attention to the essence of joy around you.
Such as
Mallard ducks floating in harmony with Damflask's ripples
Hornbeams swaying to 'flores' by Hermanos Gutierrez
Spume's embrace on Celtic sea's doorstep.
Eventide sun sipping French martinis on bamboo sofas,
honouring the day.

You Faded

I first saw you on a bus,
sat two rows in front
wearing a black leather jacket.
Your gentle presence intrigued me.

I tried to get your attention
with little success.
So, I stored my fascination in a room
in my heart: *'to be continued'*

Dancing in a nightclub
with fate on my right
destiny on my left
You finally noticed me.
Our bodies synced as one
moving rhythmically
to the sound of wild thoughts.

A week later,
siting on your bed in a blue dimly lit room
we discovered mirrors for the first time,
our conversations, effortless

I opened your ears to the soothing sound of
Afro blues, Kokoroko and Ibrahim Maalouf.
Traded embarrassing childhood stories
from our home countries.
Relived the moments that sculptured us.

In my heart,
I was ready move you from *'to be continued'*

into the *'crush'* room
Until three days later,
when I saw you kiss her.
My heart skipped a beat.
I blinked. you faded.
And couldn't make eye-contact with me.

You are now a resident of the *'trash'* room
But all I needed was eye contact.
Signalling me to make you a resident
of the *'Friend zone'* instead.

POEMS BY WARDA YASSIN

OFF THE SHELF FESTIVAL OF WORDS

WARDA YASSIN is an award-winning British born Somali poet and secondary school teacher based in Sheffield. She was a winner of the 2018 New Poets Prize for her debut pamphlet *Tea with Cardamom* (New Poets List, 2019). Her poetry has been published in places like *The North*, *Magma* and *Oxford Poetry*, and anthologised in *Verse Matters* (Valley Press), *Anthology X* (Smith|Doorstop), *Halfway Smile* & *Surfing the Twilight* (Hive). She won the 2020 Womens Poet Prize and was the former Sheffield Poet Laureate from 2020-2022. She is a member of Hive poetry collective.

Thank you to my beautiful family and friends who give me the spirit & joy to write. May Allah always protect you. Thank you to Vicky Morris for your guidance and mentorship , and to my chosen family and poetry community (Hive). Thank you also to Suzannah Evans, the Poetry Business and the Off The Shelf team for your faith in me and for this opportunity to publish alongside Danaé and Silé.

Cover author photo by Marc Baker.

Cavendish Court

She keeps inviting me in. Won't understand why
I can't walk through the door with a blue bag
filled with henna (it has to be the dry, green henna)
and a fresh cotton dress. Won't understand why
I can't massage her knees anymore with blackseed oil,

that I'm dangerous now. I stand by the front window,
laugh at her laugh through this prism of love. I ask her
of her day and she recounts routine, and phone calls
home, the floods in Burcao, how the city flows
backwards into the villages, and when she talks of her

daughter, chides her grandsons, I hear in her voice
she is chief of her household again, Hurricane Aisha.
Drinking too much tea, cardamom, ginger,
too much sugar. Sundus' chuckle steams the pane,
my eyes are glassy portholes. I know she forgets things

but never her salah, wudu in the kitchen sink.
I know she sleeps less so the nights are longer.
Inside, I catch my father slouched over
the coffee table, handpicking the bone of dates.
Her arms are soft olive branches and I distract her

when she reaches out. Something in me
comes undone. I think of how love can take
form in a face. How it stands there on the other side
of glass. Here, we are small mirrors, of each other.
Sundus and I, in a fishbowl of youth and before we go,

the same advice – *be wary of boys who don't walk*
through the front gate, remember, you have a good mother,
good father, don't be seen in bad places and find Allah
everywhere. I leave carrying an empty Sainsbury bag,
her duas filtering the street, guiding me home.

A Sonnet for Sheffield

This city is an open-palmed sanctuary, a realm
for wayfarers with henna-tipped fingers. This city
shines like flints of steel in the Maghrib light.
Her sheaf fringe finds softness and forgiveness
in everything. The hilly slopes of her body cover
the losses in her bones. She murmurs an abundance
of languages, a whirlwind of banter.
This city is the clasp, the blaring of the Adaan,
Fargate's solitude on Christmas morning,
Ayeeyo's Janazah in a strange but familiar land.
Tightly-pressed terraces yawning into winter nights.
This city is my city and she chose me to stay.
I will stay long after I leave, held
in the arms of its babbling streams.

Somaliland

Rope hair hangs from kuffis. His sapped face
glints with gold. There is a gap

between his teeth. How I long to live there,
privy to a kinder place, where hands are formed

by the love of daughters. Where children master
the languages of God and Mathematics

and after curfew, women sing forbidden gabaays.
We see a shepherd in his movements.

In his fists, diplomats nursing the burnout
of a loyal heart. He is the man

who stayed behind, nicknamed Ifiso,
honouring his first son as Mohammed.

From here, I watch his body skin itself
of loss, grow into a new life overseas.

Oh, how I long to put him on the map.

This very real thing.
        This shoe-horned boy.
                This black man of an island.

Summer of Year 9

The night they battered my father metres from where I sat,
watching Nightmare on Elm Street with my new cousins,
there had been a casuumad feast fit for a wedding.

He walked their father home, then hammered
my mother's fears onto our front door. My father – a man
of suits & algebra, from Sheikh International Boarding School,

a village boy of one real mother, tucked in a Burton shirt,
who only became black in 1990, when war smothered home
into a jar of fire – returned to us full-walleted,

face charred, berry red and ivory. I watched him call
the ambulance himself. My brother Jihad chastening –
Awo, stop crying. The neighbourhood boys pressing

down on my mother's shoulders. *Close the front door.*
Later that night, my father will measure
the exact distance of glass from his right eye,
whisper *Allahu Akbar* to the back of a pillow.

What Ahmed told me in GCSE English

War is not that deep. Wallah these poets are moving mad in this anthology. It's not about fishes, grandfathers, or holding a photo of somebody else's death. There are no similes to compare it to. When they bombed my secondary school, it was summer every day and we discovered you can find footballs in rubble. We kicked them across powdery streets like the Kirby you play here. Always keeping close tally. Nobody argued about collecting balls from behind knee length fences or a neighbour's zaytoon tree. I remember my mother stopped sleeping through the dhur siesta, and her eyes looked like small buttons whenever she watched me win.

The Glow Up

Now you work in a factory and mutuals say
he's on the straight and narrow. I say *no
he's funny business*, but here you are telling me
not to read The Star, that the worst of you
isn't the rest of your life. My father would say
*how can we go before Allah riddled with fault
asking for forgiveness when we do not forgive?*
I want to be the one not to judge what you did,
catch myself distracted by the way your body
is a climbing frame for my baby cousin, her tiny fists
pulling at your Martin Lawrence ears, the way
you pronounce my name. But all I can see
is the other boy lying on the floor being kicked
over and over, his hands spidering
the cave of his stomach,
how he helmeted his skull. And you
not stopping till you were stopped.

Now your weightless hands reach for mine,
and I see your palms flash cherry as they dangle
a life before a body. Why didn't you stop?
The same mutuals called me a *bitch*
said *people change, you're not anything.* But
you didn't stop until someone found you,
what if they never found you?
My father again *this dunya seeks redemption,
but never gives it back.* I know, I know.
Still, if only you stopped. If only
I didn't think about you all summer. The light
you cast over our city. If only you didn't
let it reach me.

Dunya: world in Arabic

When Andrea comes to paint me

there'll be no daylight lancing through
the living room window, just her demand
for the telly on. She can't work in silence.
I'll sit there like unhandled clay, waiting
for her to soften and sculpt me, watch her
assemble tools, Saturn ring-light holding me
in its orbit. Then she'll stand back, hour-glass
the air with hands, start gassin' me up
(though I came with a mirror-full of complaints)
like *your skin – unreal, your figure – unreal.*
All aquamarine eyelids, Ruby-Roo lips,
an island girl with locks silked and set –
Friday-night-ready before breakfast.
Me just there letting Andrea make summits
of sparse brows, marvelling as she mixes
my skin on the back of her hand: *Fenty, Mac,
Bobbi Brown.* Diamond-buffing high-rise cheeks,
standing back again, thumbs still moulding me.
By the time my lips are lined with *Sin,*
she knows someone else has arrived
in the little pocket mirror I'm clutching. I peacock
the swivel chair, liking the way my eyes flash
a dare to Andrea's camera phone magic wand.
Unreal, unreal! She riffs. Jamaican alchemist.
She's spun this girl into looking bad, as in
good bad. My pictures of the year
will be taken tonight. I'm the shoulder blades
of a slow dance. A sunrise over high tide.
A gold cord pulled taut up my spine. A highway
about to be dropped on this city.